FIND THE ALPHABET LETTERS IN PICTURES OF HINGHAM

Hingham

From A to Z

By Gael Daly

Illustrated by Gregory and Gael Daly

Discover an 8 letter word that begins with A and ends with Z!!
(see page 31 for the answer)

ISBN: 978-0-9825854-1-2
Hingham From A to Z ©
Digitally reproduced in 2009 by
CONVERPAGE
23 Acorn Street
Scituate, MA 02066
781-378-1996

Hingham

from A...

...to Z!

**Dedicated to the memory of our nephew
Robert K. "Bobby" Daly.**

He loved Hingham.

With sincere appreciation to my daughter Andrea for her inexhaustible patience and her computer expertise, to my son Gregory for contributing illustrations to enhance the text, and to Justine Thurston for agreeing to read and critique the book.

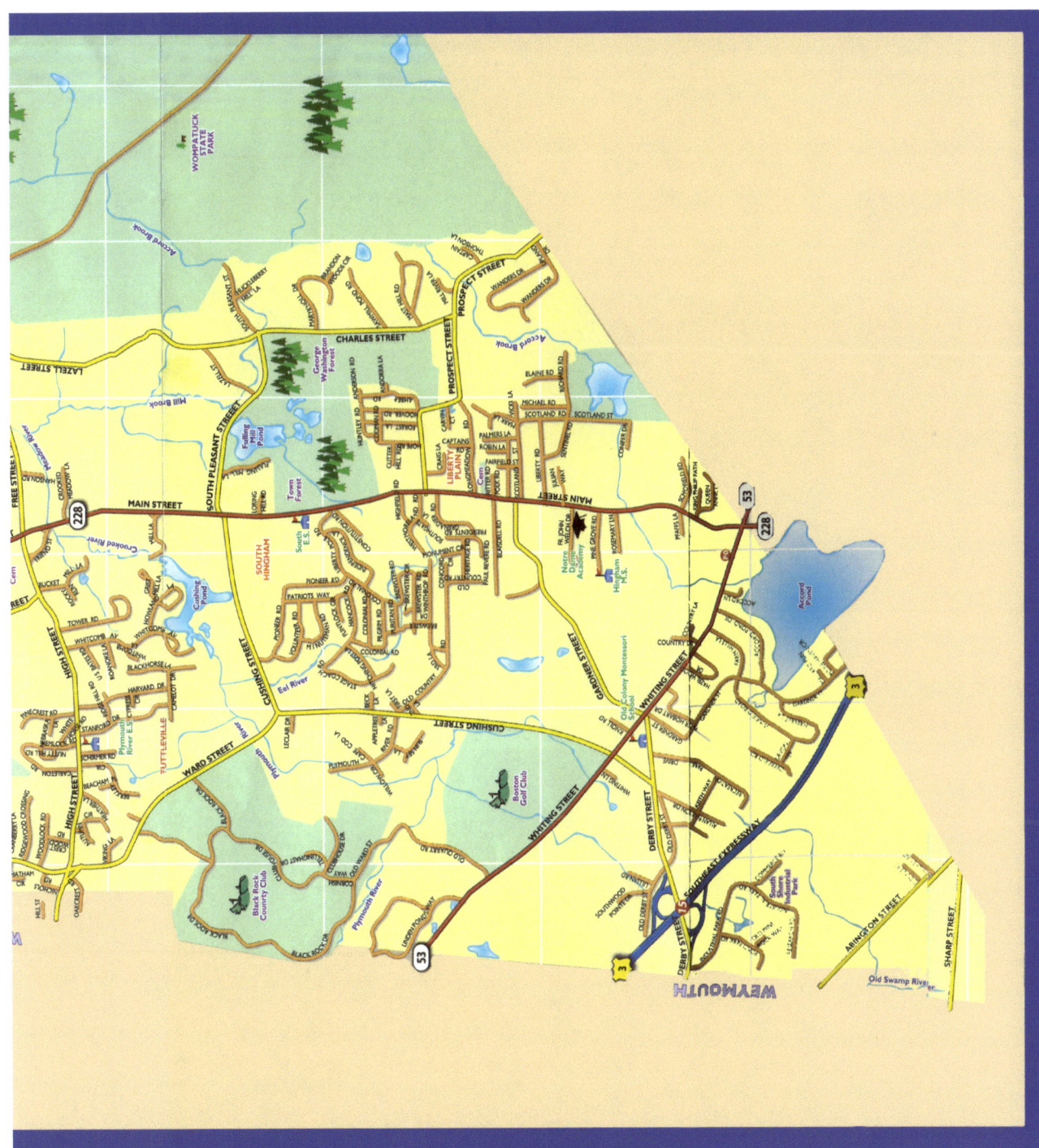

A a

Hingham Is About...

Ancestors

Many of Hingham's first settlers came from Hingham, England between 1633 and 1637. Led by Puritan minister Peter Hobart, family names included Lincoln, Hersey, Rust, Tuttle, Walton, Osborn and Fearing, all of whom were granted land in 1635. Many descendents live in Hingham today.

Art and Architecture

The Annual Arts Walk highlights Hingham's artistic and cultural life. Music, painting, poetry, and crafts are featured. Colonial and Victorian architecture can be seen throughout town.

Athletics

Go Harbormen!

B b

Hingham Boasts...

Bare Cove
is the name given by the early settlers. On September 2, 1635 the name was changed to Hingham and the town was established as the 12th town in Massachusetts. Today Bare Cove Park is a wildlife sanctuary and public recreation area along the Weymouth Back River.

Beautiful gardens
are found on both public and private property throughout town.

Beach
Hingham's main bathing beach is located next to Monument Park on Hingham Harbor.

Hingham Cherishes . . .

Children
Hingham offers children many opportunities for education, enrichment and entertainment. Children can take advantage of the natural and historic wonders that make Hingham unique.

Colonial past
Early settlers immigrated to find personal and economic freedom.

Community Center
The Community Center is the site of classes and activities for all ages. It is a social hub of the town.

![photo of bench against brick wall with ivy]

Hingham is Dedicated to . . .

Diversity
of creed and culture

Devotion
to duty, family and country

Development and Progress
From Colonial times to the present Hingham has continued to grow and change, always respecting the past and planning for the future.

E e

Hingham Enjoys . . .

Excellent schools
both public and private

Eating
at ethnic food restaurants

Entertainment
Broad Cove Ballroom, now Broad Cove Auction Hall, was a famous night spot. Gentlemen paid 7¢ and women were admitted free. Loring Hall, The Atlantic Symphony Orchestra, and South Shore Conservatory are some of today's popular entertainment venues.

Hingham is Famous for . . .

Founding Fathers
including such names as Hobart, Peck, Smith, Leavitt, Bates, Cushing, Loring, Lincoln and Fearing.

Fourth of July Celebration
featuring a parade, road race, pancake breakfast, music and fire works.

Farming, Fishing and Foresting
which were the primary occupations of the colonists.

G g

Hingham has Good . . .

Geography

Situated on the Atlantic Ocean, Hingham has a land area of 22.59 square miles. It is located approximately 14 miles southeast of downtown Boston, Massachusetts. Hingham borders Cohasset and Scituate to the east, Norwell and Rockland on the south, Weymouth on the west and Boston Harbor to the north.

Growth

residential, commercial and recreational.

Government

consists of a town administrator, three selectmen and an open town meeting.

Cornelius Nye House, North Street

Hingham Has . . .

Historic Homes

The homes on North Street were built over the course of four centuries. Hingham's six historic districts assure that the historic architecture and landscapes will be preserved.

Harbor

Circular, deep and protected by three islands, Button, Sarah and Langley, Hingham harbor became a major port of entry and fishing port. During WWII, 150 acres at the harbor were taken by the Navy for a shipyard.

History

Hingham was colonized by religious dissenters from southwest England in 1633.

Hingham Includes . . .

Industry
Early industries included agriculture, shipbuilding, fishing, trading in lumber, milling, and shoemaking. Barrel making and cordage led to the nickname "Bucket Town."

Indians
Wampanoag Indian chief Josiah Wompatuck sold Hingham to the settlers in 1665.

Immigrants
An immigrant is a person who moves to another country. The settlers were the town's first immigrants. Over the years immigrants from many countries including Europe, Asia and South America settled in Hingham.

J j

Hingham's Joy . . .

Journey
Settlers left Hingham, England for a better, freer life.

Justice
Chief Justice of MA William J. Cushing designed the Massachusetts court system and made slavery illegal in Massachusetts.

Journal
Daniel Cushing and George M. Lincoln recorded early history and town gossip.

K k

Hingham Knows . . .

King Philips War
In the 1675-1676 Indian rebellion five Hingham homes were burned and John Jacob was slain. The town was protected by three forts, one on Fort Hill, one in the cemetery and one on a plain about a mile from the harbor.

Company K
5th Regiment mustered and were sent to France in 1917.

Knuckleballer
Tim Wakefield of the Red Sox is a notable Hingham resident

L l

Lincoln Day
celebrates the lives and deeds of early Revolutionary War hero and Secretary of War, General Benjamin Lincoln and Abraham Lincoln, 16th president of the United States. Ancestors of both men were among Hingham's earliest settlers.

Hingham loves . . .

Lobsters
are a favorite food in town

Liberty
Hingham has participated in every U.S. war for liberty.

Hingham Means . . .

Military

Due to its Indian and French neighbors, every colonial town had a military organization. The result was a well-trained citizen soldiery.

Manufacturing

Some early mills became factories for the manufacture of barrels, masts, sails, plows, leather and woolen goods. During WWII the Bethlehem Hingham Shipyard mass produced 227 ships at an average rate of 6 ships per month.

Main Street

During WWII Eleanor Roosevelt visited Hingham. She considered it a 'typical' American town. In her book, *This is America*, she wrote "This is the most beautiful main street in America."

N n

Hingham Notes . . .

Navy
The Naval Ammunition Depot and the Hingham Shipyard made the U.S. Navy the largest landowner in Hingham during WWI and WWII.

Nike Missile
was housed on Turkey Hill during the Cold War. The Nike was an anti-aircraft radar controlled missile.

North Street
is one of Hingham's oldest and most historic streets. It runs from Beal Street to Route 3A.

O o

Hingham's Old . . .

Old Ordinary

Built around 1650, Old Ordinary was originally the home of Joseph Andrews, then an inn and tavern serving pints and quarts– hence "mind your p's and q's." Landscaped by Frederick Law Olmstead, it is now a museum owned by the Hingham Historical Society.

Old Derby Academy

Endowed by Madam Sarah Derby, Old Derby Academy was incorporated in 1784. It was among the first coeducational schools in the States. Tuition was to be paid in firewood. Presently it is the headquarters of the Hingham Historical Society.

Old Ship Church

on Lincoln Street was built in 1681. Its roof and ceiling resemble an upside down ship's hull. This wooden church is the oldest meetinghouse in continuous ecclesiastical use in the United States. Early town meetings were held in this building.

Hingham is Proud of . . .

Puritans
were dissenters from the Anglican Church who wanted to make the Church of England simpler in its forms and stricter about morality. The Puritans immigrated to the colonies to practice their religion freely and to form their own government.

Patriots
are the men and women from Hingham who zealously support their country.

Progress
Hingham has grown from a fishing and farming community into an affluent town. Hingham is rich in culture. It offers opportunities for education, recreation and growth, while continuing to respect and preserve its past.

Q q

**Hingham's Priority is
   Quality of Life . . .**

Queen Anne's Corner
on the Hingham/Norwell Line was originally a crossroads established by the native Indians. The corner is named after Anne Whiton who kept a tavern in the area. The tavern later became The Whiton House Restaurant.

Quilts
are bedcovers made with fabric, filled with down, then stitched together in lines or patterns. Quilts made in colonial times still can be seen today.

Quaint
Hingham is often considered quaint because of its historic character and charm and the colonial homes on quiet, tree-lined streets.

Hingham Remembers . . .

Revolutionary War

Three Hingham men helped dump tea into Boston Harbor during the Boston Tea Party on March 5, 1773. It was a key event leading to the American Revolution. Major General Benjamin Lincoln led the Hingham Militia into the war. Over 600 Hingham men served in the Revolutionary War against the British.

Reservations

are lands preserved and maintained for recreation and open space. Hingham reservations include World's End, Weir River Farm, and Whitney and Thayer Woods.

Rosie the Riveter

represents the American women who produced munitions and materials in the war factories during WWII.

S s

Hingham
Is Special for . . .

Streets
The street names in Hingham tell the story of the town. Lincoln, Derby, Hobart, Beal and King Philip are but a few names of those who influenced Hingham's history. North, South, Main, Fulling Mill, Garrison, Glacier and Constitution, help locate different areas of town or honor important events.

Shipbuilding
was one of the town's first industries and was of major importance to the success of the United States during WWII.

South Shore Country Club
has facilities for golf, hiking, swimming and tennis. Sledding in winter makes the South Shore Country Club a year-round recreation area.

Tt

Hingham Treasures . . .

Turkey Hill
is 62 acres of conservation land, in the northern part of town. Its 187 foot summit affords magnificent views of the Weir River and Hingham Harbor.

Trees
In the year 1640 legislation was enacted forbidding the cutting of trees due to the necessities of training and defense against Indian fighters. For 20 years Hingham has been declared a "Tree City USA."

Transportation
consists of bus, commuter boat, highways and railroad.

United States Constitution
Rev. Daniel Shute from South Hingham was a member of the 1780 convention that drafted the State Constitution and was on the Massachusetts committee that ratified the Constitution of the United States.

Hingham Understands . . .

United Nations
In 1945, World's End was considered as a site of the United Nations headquarters.

Unitarian Universalists
The Old Ship Church is the meetinghouse of the Unitarian Universalists congregation.

Hingham Values . . .

Village

Early village life was based on location, leadership, customs, religious beliefs, and the necessity for protection. Some Hingham villages were Hingham Center, Downer Landing, South Hingham, Glad Tidings (or Upper) Plain, Liberty Plain, Tuttleville and Queen Anne's Corner.

Veterans

are men and women who fought to defend their country's freedom. Veteran's Day is a day set aside to honor our veterans. In Hingham it is generally celebrated on the 11th day of the 11th month at the 11th hour with a ceremony at the Veteran's Memorial.

Victory Gardens

During WWII over 20 million Americans grew their own vegetables as an act of patriotism. Planting and preserving their crops allowed valuable resources to go toward the war effort.

W w

Hingham is Welcoming . . .

World's End

The 251 acre peninsula overlooking Hingham Harbor was landscaped by Frederick Law Olmstead in 1890. Rejected as a home for the United Nations Secretariat building and later as the site for a nuclear power plant, it has been preserved since 1965 as conservation land. This area of tree lined paths, rolling hills and rocky shoreline, maintained by the Trustees of Reservations, is ideal for outdoor recreation.

Whitney and Thayer Woods

is a 320 acre reservation adjacent to Turkey Hill and across from Weir River Farm. Along the 10 miles of trails are masses of rock deposited by the glaciers, Ode's Den and the secluded American holly grove. It is an excellent place for biking or hiking.

Wompatuck State Park

Visiting Wompatuck is an adventure. Formerly the Hingham Naval Ammunition Depot Annex, military bunkers, old military buildings and abandoned railroad can be explored. Connected by trails to The Whitney and Thayer Woods, Wompatuck State Park is a 287 acre recreation area good for camping, cycling, fishing, hunting, hiking, horseback riding, and snowmobiling. Free spring water can be obtained at Mt. Blue.

Hingham eXpects . . .

Xenial

is an ancient Greek word pertaining to hospitality, especially between host and guest. It speaks of gifts and the relationship to strangers. In Colonial times xenial relationships existed between different villages and between the Indians and settlers.

eXcellence

is to be strived for in school, sports, and life.

X

X is the Roman numeral for the number 10, so Super Bowl 43 is written XLIII and Hingham's 375th anniversary is CCCLXXV.

Y y

Hingham Yankees . . .

Yacht

Hingham Yacht Club on Crow Point, established in 1895, is a family oriented sailing club. It is noted for its junior sailing program, especially the Hingham Bay Junior Regatta.

Yankee

is a nickname given to an early settler or a native New Englander.

Yuletide

Christmas in the Square is a Yuletide tradition in Hingham. Santa arrives in a quaint fire engine. Hayrides, music, and caroling highlight the festivities as friends and neighbors meet to celebrate the joy of the season.

Z z

Hingham is Zealous About its History . . .

Zone

The earth is divided into 24 time zones. Hingham is in the Eastern Time Zone. It is in the North Temperate Zone. Since the sun is never directly overhead, temperatures range from warm to cool and there are 4 seasons.

Zoo

Penniman Hill Farm on Whiting Street, grows and sells herbs and flowers and has a free family petting zoo.

Zip Code

The US Post Office devised the 5 digit Zip Code system to facilitate the delivery of mail. Hingham's Zip Codes are 02043 and 02044. The first zero is for the Northeast. The "20" indicates the regional center. The last two numbers tell the specific post office.

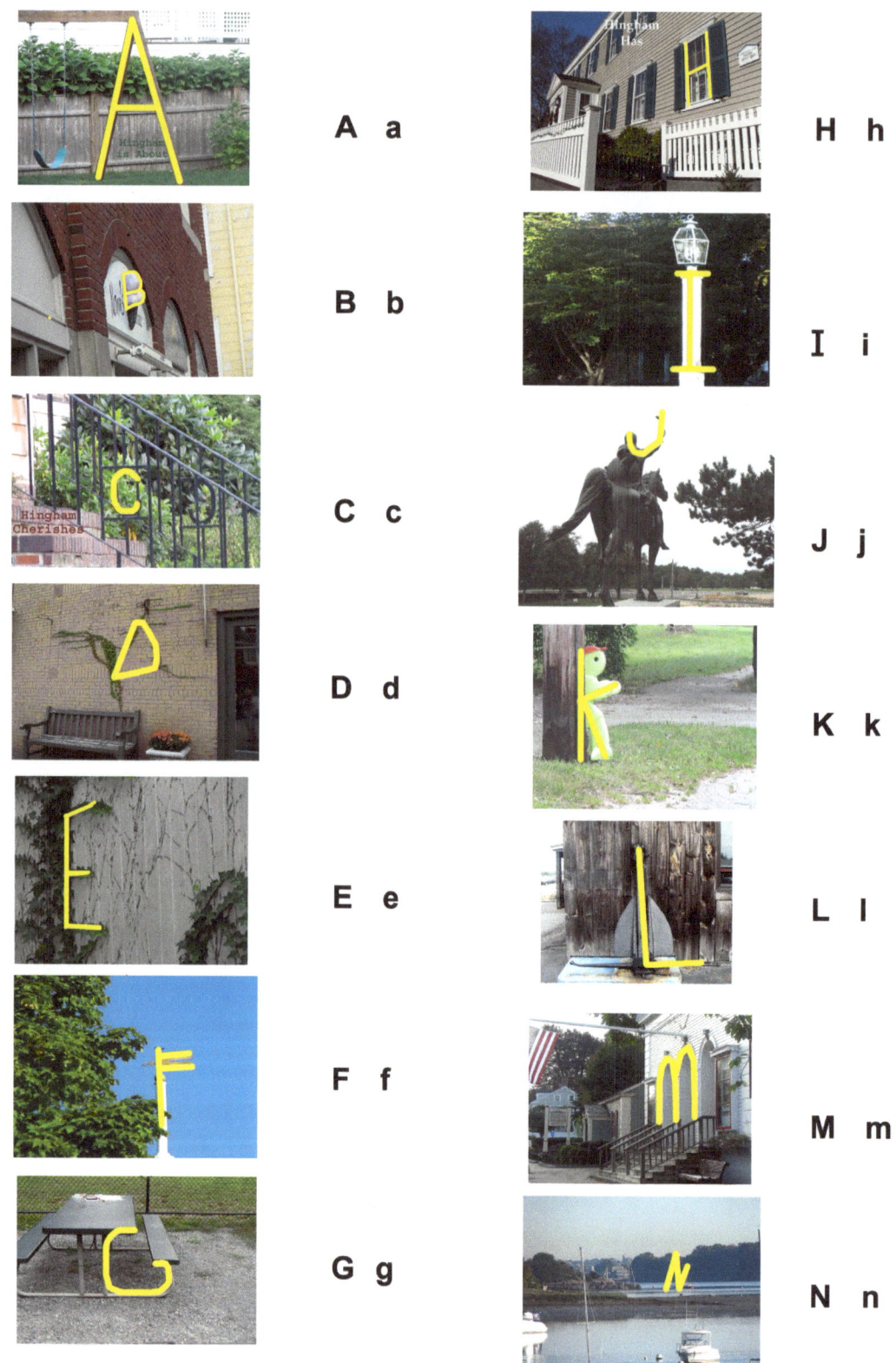

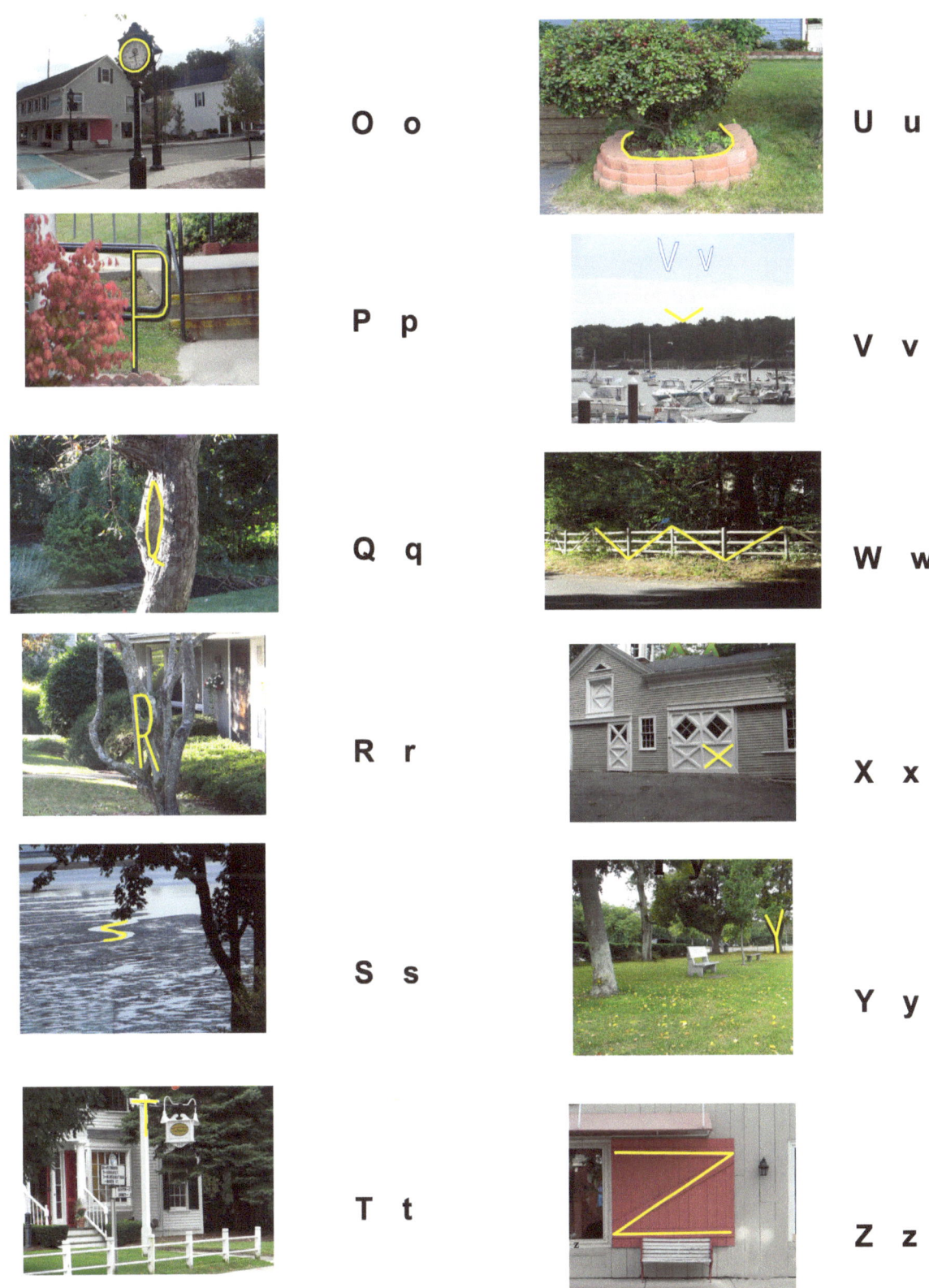

Gael (Sullivan) Daly has been coming to the South Shore for over fifty years. She now enjoys Scituate as a summer resident with her husband Timothy. Their eight children and fifteen grandchildren love to visit and enjoy the South Shore's fun and beauty.

As an Elementary School Reading Specialist for over 35 years, Gael shared her love of Children's Literature and reading with hundreds of students and numerous colleagues. Concept Books have long been a favorite genre as she has marveled at the many different shapes and forms ABC books can take.

For Gael, it was a joy writing and photographing *Hingham From A to Z*! She is also the author of *Scituate from A to Z* and *Miami Lakes from A to Z*. "Wandering through the alphabet with my readers is both a privilege and a pleasure."

"Alphabet" is an 8 letter word that begins with A and ends with Z!!

Thank you to Mrs. Travers' 4th Grade Class at Spring Street School in Shrewsbury, MA for finding that "Alcatraz" is another answer to this riddle.

If you think you have another answer, please email it to me at: abcbook@comcast.net.

www.ingramcontent.com/pod-product-compliance
Lightning Source LLC
Chambersburg PA
CBHW041537040426

42446CB00002B/132